I KNOW YOU ARE A MAN,
but I Am a Woman

Shelle

authorHOUSE®

AuthorHouse™
1663 Liberty Drive
Bloomington, IN 47403
www.authorhouse.com
Phone: 1-800-839-8640

First published by AuthorHouse 10/9/2010

ISBN: 978-1-4520-9014-6 (e)
ISBN: 978-1-4520-9013-9 (sc)
ISBN: 978-1-4520-9012-2 (hc)

Library of Congress Control Number: 2010915081

Printed in the United States of America

This book is printed on acid-free paper.

Dedications

This book is dedicated to all my ladies who are going through so many issues on any given day. Keep your heads up, and things will only get better with time. Just stay prayed up; the big man is listening. To all my men who have the courage to love, protect, provide, and care for us, I really appreciate men who know their place and act on it in a positive way. Thanks for being in our lives when you have blessed us with your beautiful offspring. Thanks for being a real father, husband, and friend; we as women really need this. Thanks for understanding us when we do not even understand ourselves. Ladies, we have so much power; we just need to figure out how to use it.

This book is also dedicated to my mom, who went through hell and high water to get to where she is today. To my son, who is my miracle every day. He is like a bundle of joy and life in the same breath. To my father, who is a gentle spirit who smiles and stays positive through the pains and aches of his body. Daddy, I will always be your little girl. To my future husband, thank you so much for accepting me in all of my mess. Thank you for loving me even when I did not deserve it. Thank you for being so gentle and kind to me and my family. Thank you for being my hero, and now I know what it means when they say, "Man is created in God's image." That must have meant you. I love you always.

Finally, this book is dedicated to everyone who reads and takes into consideration some of the experiences I have been through. Maybe some of my sorrows and pains can help you figure out how to get through. Thank you for taking time to read this book. I promise there will be more to come.

Contents

INTRODUCTION
To All My Ladies and Men

This book was written by a young lady who has had many, many sorrows in her life. She has been through many storms. It started at birth and continued until now. She has managed to make it through, even when it was very hard to see her way. She has gone through her many phases of life with the help of the men whom she was created from. Some of the men have been a strong force in her life, but others have been her downfall. She has had many addictions that she just could not live without. She thought that she needed them in her life. Actually, her life was being defined by them. She would cater to them whenever they would call to her too. She never minded that they were only around her for the things she could do for them. She would pay their bills, buy them cars, pay their rent, put money into their pockets, take on their children, and keep their children for them. This woman would do anything to keep their company. This is what made her happy. She kind of knew that they did not mean her any good, but she could say that she had a man. Does this sound familiar to some? Women seem to put so much work into empty houses. We will love on someone that just does not give a damn whether we are breathing or not. We will love on someone who will not check on us if we do not have two nickels to rub together, but will come and check on us if our bank accounts are full of nickels. This is so amazing to me. How is it that we keep on letting this happen? After all, we have some amazing powers that we are blessed with, but we refuse to use them. As a matter of fact, we give our powers away on a given day.

CHAPTER ONE
I Am Woman

I was created from a man for a man to bond and build a family with. I was not placed here on this earth to be alone. I was placed here to be fruitful and to multiply for my man. God created me so that I can be a helpmate to my man. He created me to be a mother, daughter, sister, aunt, nurse, secretary, college student, and so on, and most important of all, a wife. Women can be anything that we put our minds to. We may often come off as the weaker sex, because we look very fragile, but we are so strong in so many things. For some of us, our strength comes from a higher power up above, and for some other women, our power comes from a man who has no clue who we are and what we are made up of. You will often find that we have learned to have strong faith through our mothers and grandmothers. We have learned to be very prayerful in all things. Especially in the hard times, we may pray even harder. We as woman are very gentle and kind. We were born to be everything that is love. We are nurturers in every aspect of our souls. We were born to have this unique quality. We are always ready to trust anyone outside of us, especially the opposite sex, until that trust is shattered. We are always ready to love the opposite sex unless they betray us with all of their mind games. You know, it's funny how sometimes we still can manage to love a man after the betrayal, but when the shoe is on the other foot, he tends to shun away from us with disgust. I was just wondering where exactly it is written that men should do whatever they want without thinking of their women's feelings? What is the name of that book? No one ever realizes that love is a gift and that when you find it, you should hold onto it for dear life. People tend to love you after you have put up with all that you can and have decided to walk away. Before, they did not realize what they had, but love miraculously shows up as soon as you start packing your bags. Now how ironic is that?

Real love only comes down your pathway once or twice. If you pay close attention, you will know when it is real love. Some people often mistake real love for infatuation. When love comes knocking at your door, you'd better answer. It may not come in a fancy package with a ribbon tied around it. Or better yet, it may not come to you in any form that you are used to. Not the dime pieces, not the drop-dead gorgeous female, not even the different body measurements that you are used to—not meeting any of the requirements that you have laid out for a perfect person. Love may just come and hit you right in the heart. If a woman gives you her heart and everything else, you need to learn to accept it with pride. It's a blessing when you accept a woman's heart. It's like a breath of fresh air knowing that you have someone who is down for you. She is someone who would die for you if you asked her to. Well, not literally, but you get the idea.

When you start to ignore us and take us for granted, this is the start of a silent war, because we can't seem to comprehend the emotional and physical neglect. We will not be able to accept the fact that you have lost your mind and forgotten who has stood by your side through thick and thin. When these things are taken for granted, this is when you start to see a slow and painful change in us. It may not matter to you in the beginning, but eventually you will get the picture. It will be like a thief in the night. You will not have a clue who just robbed you and took everything that you took from us. When we first meet you, we are so excited and willing to do whatever it is that you demand of us. Actually we are at your very command. You have been granted your own little personal woman who can be anything and everything to you if you just let her. I guess you could say we worship you in the beginning. You mean more to us than we mean to ourselves. It is a shame to say that, but it is the truth. We are somewhat peculiar in the beginning because we are trying to figure you out. We are constantly asking ourselves a series of questions: Is this man with me for my money? Is he only with me for sex that he is not getting anywhere else? Is he just trying to use me for a place to stay? What is his purpose for wanting to kick it with me? I have been a victim of many men just wanting me for money and sex. I remember a time when I was receiving AFDC, which is public aid for low-income individuals. Even though I was receiving $236 a month, my guy wanted $200 of it. Not having a clue, I would only give him half of it, because I was under the impression that he was going to take care of me with it. It was a joke. Yeah, the last laugh was on me. He was spending my little money on other females that he thought were much better than me. Over the years my income increased. The more my income grew, the more men I could find. They would flock to me like flies would flock around shit—imagine that. It is a shame, but it is so true. And a man wanting to have sex with me because he had nowhere else to turn was turning out to be a normal thing. I did not know any better at the time that these men were just using me as a sperm depository. After a while I got used to being used in this way; I may not have gained the man himself, but I did gain temporary affection. A woman needs affection, and sometimes we have to go get it by all means necessary, even if that means self-humiliation. I often think of the things that we go through just to be touched. To some men, cuddling is out of the question. I have noticed that they do not mind cuddling when they are grabbing you by your head. Ladies, you know what I mean. They grab you by your head when they want their dicks sucked.

I am a humanitarian by nature, so my instincts used to automatically kick in whenever someone needed a place to stay. I have always been the type that if I found out that you were a paycheck from being homeless, I would be your superhero.

I would often make the necessary adjustments in my life just so I could give you the best that I have to give. Some of my guys did not grasp this concept. They thought this was owed to them. I can count the many times when I gave my men a place to stay and they started acting out and disrespecting my home. A warm and cozy home I provided to them out of the kindness of my heart. I did not ask them for any money or any kind of assistance, and they still had the audacity to run out and kick it with some other female. What the hell is that about?

I believe that everyone crosses your path for a reason. Maybe the reason is good or bad, but whatever the reason, it should be a learning experience. Whenever someone new comes into my life, I take a really hard look at the gentleman from many different angles. I need to know if he has arrived in my life just because, or if he is really being sincere. Or is he just interested in me out of convenience? I have been destroyed and ripped apart in many ways, just as many other women have been, but I am proud to say that I have not been scorned as badly as some. I just took everything as a painful learning experience. Many of my sisters feel scorned, and they have reason to. Because if you are giving everything to that man that you possibly can give, then what the hell is left? Some women will never trust another man for as long as they live. Their hearts have been destroyed and torn beyond recognition. I admit I have had a few too many guys and one female in my life, but half of the guys were just something that I needed at the time. It was not because I needed a relationship. It was just because I had a problem with addiction. I will get into my addictions more later in the book. Men are a beautiful thing, but beautiful does not always mean good for you. These bodies of art are very dangerous when it comes to matters of the heart. Once they know that you are into them, they show off and play so many games because they know they have you at your most vulnerable moment. Before they really know that you are into them, they treat you with such dignity and respect. They treat you like you are a queen and they are your king. I guess this is because they are really trying hard to impress you with what really is not true.

As a matter of fact, as human beings we often bring about our representatives instead of our true selves. We want to make sure that this new person does not know who we are, because if he really knew about us, he would not give us the time of day. We do not want anyone to be turned off by us. Like they say, the first impression is the lasting impression. I guess this is true, because this is the way we present ourselves in any given situation. For example, when interviewing for a job or meeting a new friend, a new Realtor, or anyone we want to impress, we are on top of bringing out our fake selves, because we are scared to death of people being turned off by our true identity. I guess this is the price we pay for living in a perfect world. Yeah, right. The society that we live in has us so brainwashed that being our true selves is just not tolerated. There are so many products and plastic surgery to help us hide behind a mask. Being someone other than ourselves is a billion-dollar industry. I would think that it would be cheaper to be ourselves, but it would cause conflict with the rest of the world.

I have been guilty of bringing out my representative so many times. When I do this, I often forget who I really am. The reason I bring out my representative is because at times my situation may call for it. I may need to bring out my representative so that I will not have to deal with whatever is going on at the time. It is like my shield from the reality of the Shelle show. I have suffered so many times at the hand of ridicule. I have been laughed at, lied to, and talked about by many. I have been made to feel that I am not good enough to even be alive and walk the earth with the rest of the human species. I have been made to feel that I am not a beautiful young lady. I have been made to feel that I am not, and never will be, as attractive as the next lady. Basically I have had no self-esteem because it was never established. I guess when a man told me that I was nothing, I believed him. I guess you can say that I was defining my life by whatever a man told me, not knowing that I had the power to be anything that I put my mind to. I believe some men like to play mind games with us so that we will not go following after another man who sees our true value. They are scared that we will realize that we have some value and walk away from them without looking back. Some men prey on the weak woman. They prey on her simply because they can control her and her mind. It is a fact that a way to a woman's heart is through her mind. If you have her mind, the rest will surely follow.

Some men feel that if they get someone with low self-esteem, then they can and will get whatever they want from her. What the men do not realize is that the woman is already there for him. So why try to control something that is already given to you? As I have mentioned before, men like these types of women because they can use these women for their money, car, or a place to stay where they do not have to pay any bills. Some of these women are on public assistance and can barely take care of themselves and their children, and then here comes a man with his pretty smile and nice build, and the sex is very good, and he even has a car. This is really impressive to a single mom who is lonely and has no one to hold her when she is crying in the night because she has to deal with so much stress. Sometimes it doesn't even matter if he takes her out or not. It doesn't even matter if she is paying for everything. She just wants his attention and the little affection that he can offer to her. At times it doesn't even matter if he has someone else. They say that women outnumber men anyway, so it is going to be this way, women say. I am not justifying this; I am just keeping it real. I have been guilty of going through this also. So I know what it feels like to sell your soul to the devil for a little unrealistic time. I am a very friendly young lady; I would give you the shirt off my back. I would even give you my last dime just so that you would have something to eat. I am your partner until the end. I am your ride-or-die kind of chick. I am your Bonnie, and you are my Clyde. Your income does not matter to me. I have never been one of those chicks that are with you for your job, clothes, or car, because I know that those things could be gone in a twinkle of an eye. I do not put faith in "things." I put faith in a higher power. As long as you treat me with kindness and respect, I can be your very best friend. This is all that I ask from you, *man*. This is so hard for some of you to do. The world is right there in the palm of your hands, but you choose to throw it all away on some nonsense. You choose to ignore the fact that we are so precious and sensitive. We are so emotional and rely on you to help us through. After all, we are your rib. Instead of just putting us on a plate and eating us, you should be more loving and gentle to us.

We look to you as our father figure. I will explain in more detail. When I say you are like a father figure to us, I mean that we are looking up to you the way we look to our fathers. We know that you are not our father, but this is how some of us choose you. If our father is a wonderful man, then that is the kind of man we tend to choose. If our father has abandoned us, then that is the kind of man we tend to choose. Some ladies may beg to differ, but I believe that this is so true in many instances. We need to be protected, loved, and taken in with pride. To our fathers, we are daddy's little girl, no matter how old we get. To our husbands we are the best thing since sliced bread. To our boyfriends we are supposed to be *the one* and only, working our way up the ladder to becoming much more. Men, you are supposed to take charge and be proud that someone wants to be a part of your life and give you the best that she has to give. You are supposed to protect her when you see harm coming her way. You are supposed to love her back when she is desperately seeking it. A lot of us need you and not only want you. We need to know that someone is there for us in every circumstance. I know that a lot of you guys say that you have been burned one time too many, and you will only be able to love twice and no more. What the hell is that about? So are we supposed to just put up with that and let you do whatever it is you feel like doing to us? Are we supposed to buy into that excuse that you will never be able to love again? I believe that you should tell us in the beginning that you are not going to be able to give us anything, instead of playing with our heads. Some of us can understand it better if you are honest in the beginning. What some of you are not aware of is that we have been through something too. We have been battered too, mentally and physically, to the point where half of us have turned to another woman for love. Yes, I said it; some of us have turned to other women for emotional support. But some of us have been scorned so badly that we have no emotions. We have put our guard up so high that you would have to be an astronaut to touch base with us. We think we are being so strong, but we are only getting farther from being what God has created us to be. He did not create us to be so hard and cold. He created us to be sensitive to others and gentle. I am often confused about which way I should go. I am not sure if I should show you my kind and gentle side or show you a cold and stern Shelle. I am not sure what to do at times. I am scared to give fully because I just do not think that my heart can take it. I have many battle scars that just will not heal no matter the many times that I have tried to reach out. Right now I am going through something with someone, and I just keep running into a closed door. He has built a wall so high that you would have to go into space to look over it. He uses the excuse that he was in a relationship for three years and that he was burned. I am still not sure what that has to do with me. I am into him, but he is in another universe. No matter how hard I try to let this brother know that I am here for him, he lets me know that I am not it. He has used that excuse that is so common, almost like a script out of a play. He said he has fallen twice and that he does not see that love is coming again. He says that it is going to take time to love again. My question is, does he even have a clue what love is? I believe that he is still strung out on his ex. The ex factor, as I call it. He does not even know that I exist. When he looks at me, he must see her, because he sure in the hell does not see me. I am not sure why the ex has a major role in a person's life when the ex is gone, but it often seems that you are fighting with a ghost whenever you are competing with an ex. He was in a relationship with this diva for a while and believed that they did not have anything in common, but they both sure could have fooled me. This is the reason that I cannot get through to him. He says that I am wrong, but I believe that I am so right. If you are wondering why I am sticking around, I am sticking around because I love him. I love him with every fiber of my being, but he will never know this because he does not realize it. I believe he will realize it when it is too late. I often have wondered, why do we realize what we have after it is gone? Is it because we took it for granted, or is it because we just do not care? As soon as I get rid of this disease of love for him, I will then let go. Love itself is not a disease. It's just so hard when you fall for someone who does not feel the same about you. It is so devastating when you find out that you are skipping all by yourself down a very busy highway. I know that he may not deserve my love, but I've really got it bad right now. I figure it will be a matter of time before I get to be free from disaster. Right now I am serving a sentence that I am waiting to be paroled from. This is what it feels like. I am not even sure that he even cares about the changes that I am going through. I am going through hell and back. You know the funny thing is that I know for a fact that there is someone out there who loves me unconditionally. But I choose to mess around with Satan. Ladies, you know this is how some of us get down. What's good for us we do not want, but what is bad for us we will kill a dead snake over. What is the mystery behind this? Why do we go through these self-mutilating changes? We say we are looking for love, but we are contradicting ourselves when we are chasing the wrong brother. Some women say that it's the thug in the man that keeps us going. That may be true to some, but I think it's just the man itself. We are attracted to this brother simply because of the science of chemistry. We have gotten all confused because the sex is wonderful. After all, this is a form of communication. Ladies, we all know that they are very good at this. As a matter of fact, they are very eager to communicate with us on this level. They hear every word that we moan. Isn't it a pity that this is where the communication stops for some of our men? Please, do not get me wrong. I really enjoy this way of conversation, but can you men go the extra mile and communicate with us after it's over and done? You will be able to find out so much more about your queen if you just take time out to see what is on her mind.

A lot of you think that we say the same thing over and over, but this is not true. If we do, it's because you never got the point the first time. We feel that we have to keep telling you things to give you time to get yourself together before we start thinking of leaving you. We are trying to give you a chance to save face. We are giving you a chance to realize that you may be letting the best thing that you ever had walk out with no point of return. Some of you may not care about that, because you have other women on standby. Here is a little secret: the women that are on standby are looking for the same thing that your original woman is looking for. The only difference is that the standby woman is telling you what you want to hear, and she is not giving you any grief, because she is so happy to see you whenever you both can meet. Your first lady, who is the lady of the house, she has your back and she is your teammate. She is making sure that everything is in order in the household. If all you think is that this woman is getting on your nerves, then think again. She is and has given you everything that she has to offer, and she demands respect. You need to listen to her whenever she is speaking. I know you do not want to hear this, but she knows what is best for you both. She is just trying to love you and care for you and your children. She is not trying to harm you. She is just trying to do what she has been created to do. All you have to do is love her and let her be herself. Stop being so macho and a hardass. Be easy on all of us. Realize that we have been hurt too, and we are running scared too. Stop beating us up with your words and actions. If you take the time to do the right thing by us instead of the wrong thing, then you may be onto something. Remember, treat us as you would treat your daughters. Give us plenty of protection, love, security, and much more.

CHAPTER TWO
I Am Emotional

I would like to say first that women were created to be emotional beings. We are the weaker sex, yet we are very strong when it is required of us to be. Being in love with a man takes a lot out of us on a given day. Sometimes we do not know if we are coming or going. Sometimes it feels as if we have lost control of everything. We often feel powerless when it comes to you. We are hypnotized by your unique attributes. You have your slick words and your seductive touch. You have a way of making us feel that it's all about us. I know that your intentions may not mean any harm in the beginning, but the more we spend time with each other, we know that it's not really about us. It is about what we can do for you. Some of you are so clueless about women. Some of you are right on point. I guess it depends on how many hearts you have broken before you get it right. I have heard some men tell me that they knew that they had let a good woman go, but there was nothing that they could about it at the time. They say that they did not see her standing in front of them. They saw someone else that they could not let go of in their past. This is a tragedy in itself. You are supposed to make sure that walking away is what you truly want to do before you let that special someone go. If you are sure you want that person out of your life, then do all the things necessary to make sure you are not making the biggest mistake of your life. If you do not make sure you are done for good with the ex, then you will certainly carry baggage from one relationship to another. This causes so much unnecessary drama for everyone involved. I have been guilty of sabotaging a really good relationship simply because I either did not think I deserved it, or I just did not know how to respond to something good. A lot of us are not used to anything positive and good in our lives. We are just used to the negative things that have taken place in our lives. I admit that I have messed up so many good relationships because I was damaged goods. I was battered and bruised, mentally and physically. I could not accept that someone accepted me for me.

Being damaged goods is so hard because you have to walk around like nothing and no one bothers you. You have to walk around with your representative all of the time. You cannot walk around with any signs of weakness. You are afraid that people will destroy you if they see a sign of weakness. This is not the kind of life that I choose to live. I have made up my mind to look the challenges of love straight in the eye. I may be a little scared, but I will still go forward. I will keep my head up and move on over to the next man who sees me for who I am, not what he wants me to be. I have this little saying that I always tell my men friends. When they feel like I may be too much for them, I always tell them, "Eat what you can off this plate, but pass the plate to the next man if it's too much for you." I believe that if I am too much for them, then we should agree to move on and stop wasting each other's time and energy. We should just move wherever the wind blows us. We should take what we have learned, and that is only if we have learned anything, and we should use it on our next trip on love. Some of us will never be able to love again unless we are paid a million dollars. Even then falling in love will be like pulling teeth. Some people would rather have their hearts set on fire than to fall in love again.

I think that falling in love is a privilege that is worth the pain and sorrow at the end of the journey. Love is a gift that we should learn to surrender to, instead of running from. Like Betty Wright has sung, "No Pain No Gain." This was my favorite song on her album. I was too young to understand the lyrics then, but I surely understand them now. The most painful part of the whole love thing is that we as women are the ones who are fooled. We think that we are the ones to make this man in our lives straighten up. We think that we can change him into what we want him to be. We also think that if we do everything for him in this world and beyond, he will choose us to play on his team. Boy, are some of us so wrong. I am going the extra mile now for my guy and whoo-whee, he is giving me a run for my money and then some. I love him so much that he is all I think about. I breathe him, I taste him, I just feel everything for him. He is too messed up to realize it. He finds all of the reasons to dismiss me instead of finding reasons to hold on to me. He listens to other people who think they know me. I always tell him that I do not want to hear about him and his boys who think they know me. He is not wise enough to figure out that maybe his boys may want me for themselves. After all, I am one of a kind. All women should think like this. They should lift their heads up and say, "Listen here, world, I am somebody who knows who she is and knows what she wants." I may be pretty emotional at times, but that comes with the territory of being a woman. A woman whom men should adore and worship. Men should treat us like a garden that is blossoming. If you water a garden, it continues to grow into a beautiful healthy piece of land. This is how you should treat your woman, instead of like the soil that the garden is depending on.

If you men would take the time to get to know us, I mean really know us, you would be very surprised to find out that we are not too different from you. It puzzles me how some of us get treated by the opposite sex. We are depending on you as men to carry us through this life. God has taken a rib from you so that you could have someone to be there with you—to be there as a teammate and to help you follow your dreams for the both of you. We have given up our power to you, believing that you are going to do the right thing by us. Some of you hate us so much that you would rather see us destroyed than loved.

A lot of you say that if you had not been hurt before the new woman, maybe you would give the new woman a chance to shine in her own way.

Sometimes men hate us so much that they harm us badly. They may love us for the first year of the new relationship, but then things start to get really rocky the next year and later on. Some of you can be real assholes; some of you start to be very possessive and violent toward us. I have yet to figure out why you put your hands on us. What gives you the right? What is it that justifies you slapping us around or beating the hell out of us? There is not a day that goes by that I do not remember being a victim of domestic violence from the time I was fifteen to the time I was nineteen. Instead of my king loving me, he was beating the hell out of his queen just because he felt like it. He actually felt like he had the right to do whatever he pleased; after all, he was the breadwinner at the time. He knew that the beatings would not make me leave him, because I had nowhere else to go, and besides, he was the only family that I had, since he had isolated me from my real family.

I came from a broken home where my mom was addicted to crack. Things were very crazy in our household at the time. We had little food, few material things, and little peace. I can remember at the time that we were so hungry that all we had in the house was some government cheese, powdered milk, and one egg. My mom and I had to figure out how we were going to share this one egg between three people. I can tell you so many stories that would just make your heart cry for me. But that will be in the next few chapters. Right now I will get back to the domestic violence that took place in my life at a very young age. I will dedicate a chapter solely to this issue, since there are so many women silently suffering from abuse by their men—the men that we love and trust so much.

CHAPTER THREE
Domestic Violence

Coming into the world, I had the most loving parents that one could ever dream of having—even though my mom only married my father because she felt sorry for him and that was a way of moving out of her parents' home. My mother did not realize that she had married a wonderful man, who adored her so. She took it as a game; he took the marriage for real. He did everything and anything in this world for her because he was just happy that someone wanted to be with him. If my mom even thought of something that she wanted, he would make it magically appear. He is a wonderful father in all aspects. He is always so positive, no matter the situation. His friends call him Smiley, because he is always wearing a smile. I often wondered what in this world had him smiling so much, about twenty-four hours a day. I found out that he is just always thinking of how blessed he is to be alive. My father is very gentle and quiet. He would never put a hand on you unless you were threatening him or his family. It often mystifies me how he got to be who he is with no guidance at all by a male role model. My father came from a broken home. His mother passed away when he was thirteen, and his father just did not leave anything behind but my father's name. So it just puzzles me how he continues to be a free spirit. My father has lived a lonely life. He had no brothers or sisters. He just had a whole bunch of cousins that only wanted to be bothered by him if they were going to be drinking. Even today you can't find any of his relatives. It's like he has been abandoned. He only has his children and nothing else. It often saddens me that others don't want this gentle spirit around them.

Some men blame not having a father in the home for the way that they are. I think that is a poor excuse for the stupidity that they display. Even though they may come from a broken home with no father, they still can make a difference in someone's life. They do not have to hold on to that anger and take it out on the world because their father walked away. When they get to a certain age, it is time to put the excuses down. At a certain age, they should know right from wrong. Not having a father in the home does not give them an excuse to beat the hell out of their women or children. Even having a father that was in the home but was very abusive does not give them the right to put their hands on someone else. Once they are old enough to realize that harming another individual is an absolutely no-no, they should just keep it moving if they feel the urge to lay their hands on a woman or children. It's cheaper and safer to just walk away from a volatile situation. I have heard so many excuses for why a man acts out, and none of them are valid. I often hear the classic saying, "She made me do it." Yeah, right. My response to this is that you are going to make me kill you in your sleep and then call the police and the morgue. I am not going to be a victim of a man's hand again as long as I live. I value my life as much as you value yours, so please do not put us both in a situation where one is going to jail and the other one is going straight to the morgue. This is not a threat; this is a promise.

My mom today is still as sweet as she wants to be. When I was younger, she was not that sweet. She was going through a lot of changes that I did not understand at the time. I did not understand that life could make you do some strange things that you have to question. My mom did not realize that once she walked away from my father, she was going to be dealing with some bad seeds. After she and my dad separated, she could never find that love and gentleness that she once felt. As a matter of fact, I do not believe that she has had anyone decent in her life ever since my father. It has been one roller-coaster ride after another. She has run into men that took her pretty smile for granted. They took her kindness and ran with it. They started manipulating her and making her do things to them that were unspeakable. They preyed on the fact that she did not have any self-esteem and was yearning for affection. They knew that she was an easy target for the games that they liked to play.

My mom was a survivor in all situations, whether it be good

or bad. She would do whatever she had to do to make it in this big, scary world. She would work and do whatever it took to make a living. My mom had one job that outshone them all, and that was being a lady of the night back in the seventies. As a matter of fact, a lot of women chose this occupation, just so that they could feed their families. It was not the best job in the world, and it may not have paid any insurance, but it did pay the bills and keep food on the table. This profession is not very glamorous. After a while you turn into something that you do not even recognize. It is not like a regular job where you get promotions and are recognized by your peers for a job well done. It is just a job of survival and nothing else. This profession is also a very dangerous one, because you never know what could happen to you on a given day or what lunatic you could run into. These are the risks that you have to take just to make a dollar. It is kind of like having a job working twenty-four hours with no sleep and getting paid peanuts. But like the saying goes, you have to do what you have to do to take care of your family.

With my mom doing her job, and doing it well I might add, she was raped, held up at gunpoint, beaten, and forced to do trains for little or no money at all. She went through this for so many years that she became very numb to any kind of emotions that a woman was created to feel. I often wondered how she ended up being attracted to this type of lifestyle. There were so many negative things that came with the territory of being degraded for a dollar. She got to the point that she made herself believe that she really enjoyed doing this job. She really made herself believe that she did not deserve to do any better. She began to believe that this is how love was received; however, it was through the hands of a stranger. This is exactly what I am talking about when women are deprived of the love and affection of a real man. We start to fall victim to the sick fantasies that men have about us. There is nothing wrong with having fantasies, but some fantasies should be stopped at just as a thought. My mom began to grow lifeless. Every time she clocked in on the prostituting shift, she fell into the devil's trap of sex, drugs, and videotapes. She no longer knew who she was. The only thing that she knew was that she was once Daddy's girl who got lost in a world of madness.

As I got older, the things that would come out about my mother were painfully horrifying. She had been through so much at a very young age that it followed her through her older years. The things that she had been through were insane, and when I think about it sometimes, I just silently cry for my mother. I am not sure that any average woman would be able to go through the drama she had to endure and live to talk about it. I am not saying there are no other women walking around with these kinds of horrifying secrets; I am just saying that if you hold them in without talking about it, the secrets will destroy you. I take my hat off to her and her struggles. I did not understand then, but I truly understand now all the pain and violence she went through. I did not understand what a person who doesn't have your best interest in mind could do to you. I did not understand that it only takes one person to mess up your whole entire life without any remorse. My mom was robbed and destroyed by the hands of many. She was hurt beyond recognition. She never knew that someone could treat a person so cold even when you are giving them your best.

What I am about to tell you is going to make you reach down in your past and analyze what went wrong in your own life. It will make you ask questions about who you really are and why you accept bull from others like you do. I had to reach down deep inside to find out why I was the way that I am. It was quite a surprise when I found out that the truth that I had been searching for was right there the whole time. I was looking the truth in the eye every day that I woke up. The truth was staring right back at me whenever I looked in the mirror. I guess you can say that it was a reflection of self. I have to admit that I often would not look in the mirror for fear of what I would see.

My mom grew up in a two-parent home with twelve siblings. She was the oldest girl, and she had an older brother who was more like a father to her than her own father. Her father was a mean alcoholic, who demanded that in his house, his way was the only way. There were no questions asked about anything. My grandmother was sweet, but a strict disciplinarian. Education was her focus for all of her children. She believed that with hard work and a positive attitude, you can accomplish anything in this world. I never met my grandmother. She died of complications of a stroke when I was two years old. I really wish I could have met her, because she could have given me the guidance that I needed when dealing with my life lessons. I miss her, simply because I did not get a chance to tell her I love her and that I would do my very best in whatever directions my paths may take me. She is sadly missed even more by her children.

Before my grandmother passed away, my mother and grandma would often come into great conflict. I am not exactly sure when my mom started to have conflict, but it was an ugly battle between the two whenever they did. My mom would often tell my grandmother things that she would be in denial of. My grandmother always had a hard time believing half of the things that my mother told her. I am not sure why, but I guess some of the things were too painful to hear. One incident in particular was when my mom came up pregnant at the age of fourteen and lost the baby. My mom would never tell who got her pregnant or where she conceived. My mom was between a rock and a hard place when it came to telling my grandmother the truth. She knew that telling my grandmother would do nothing but bring them further apart. My mom got pregnant again at the age of sixteen. My grandmother was furious this time. She knew she was not going to get the truth out of my mother, so she sent her straight to a home for girls. She figured that if my mom spent some time there at the home, the truth would come out eventually. The truth was so hard to tell because the one that was getting her pregnant was not supposed to even have that kind of lust for her. The truth was my mother had not only gotten pregnant, but it was rumored that she had gotten pregnant by her father. The father she trusted to protect her from harm was the one crossing the line. My mom was very developed and very beautiful. He had a little nickname for her; as a matter of fact, he had nicknames for all of his daughters. My mom's nickname was "Chanel No. 5" He would get jealous of the teenage boys who were interested in my mother. He would often punish her by taking her to vacant houses and laying newspaper on the floor and having sex with her repeatedly. He made sure that he was going to be the only man in her life. This is a very sick way of thinking. I get ill when I think of my grandfather sticking his penis inside of my mother, destroying her life forever. My mom would cry so loud for him to stop, but he never listened. She knew that if she told her mother what her father was doing to her secretly, they would come into a verbal fight. Her mother would call her a liar. Her mother would just tell her that she was fast and nasty for letting some boy around the neighborhood get into her panties. My mom suffered for so long and for so many years at the hands of her father. By the way, my mother lost that baby too. Thank goodness, because living with the physical evidence of betrayal would have been even worse than living with the mental evidence. If these babies had survived, it would have killed her, because they would have been a constant reminder. I am not even sure what would have happened to her. This could possibly explain her mental breakdowns. As she got older, she would have nervous breakdowns and had to be admitted to different facilities for the mind. I never understood what set the breakdowns off; I just know that they were very painful to watch. I loved my mom so, but when she would have these breakdowns, it would scare me so. I always knew when she was going to have one because I was always there when they started. She would definitely start showing strange behavior. She would start to act really, really strange. It was too much for a young mind to endure.

My mom's life was so complicated. No one really understood her, not even her. She just knew that she was developing behaviors that were not normal. So being promiscuous was the only way of coping with the pain and sorrow of her past. She did not have the proper guidance to help her with choosing the right man. She had no blueprint laid out for her. She had to learn on her own the hard way, whether it was by doing the necessary or the unnecessary. My heart goes out to all you ladies who have experienced heartache by any man, whether it was your father or just another man in general.

We go through so much at any given time. We are very devastated when someone we trust and respect commits violence against us. I am not sure if my grandfather ever took the time to think about what he was possibly doing to his daughter, but I am very sure that she thought about it daily. She is doing okay right now, but every now and then, she withdraws from reality. She is currently in a relationship that is going nowhere. They have been together for approximately thirty years. They have no intentions of getting married. I reckon that they are comfortable in shacking up. I just can't imagine being with someone for that long and not being married to him. See once again, this is what I mean when I say we as women will settle for anything just so we do not have to be alone. We have become so desperate and needy. I guess as long as the thing that is sitting next to us is breathing, we are in heaven. No one can tell us any different. Their relationship is like an old building that is standing but could fall apart at any given moment. She has fooled herself into thinking that she has the best thing on earth. And as far as him, he is just enjoying the ride in not having to prove himself anymore. She is putting out way more than she should for this guy. He puts out very little, and that is only because she allows him to. Men only do what we allow them to do to us. Some women beg to differ, and some say, "You know what, Shelle, you are so right." Men know that they do not have to put out much effort to make us jump. They have been blessed to be that way. We have to prove everything, that we are worthy to be in their presence. Damn, this is so sad that we just can't be equal when it comes to love. Women are so beautiful and yet treated like nothing more than ATMs, sperm depositories, and shelters. How did all of this happen? And how did all of this begin? We are at war with each other. We are constantly trying to love someone who does not have a clue, because he thinks that he is not required to love us back. Besides, he can find someone else who has low self-esteem who will not require much of him. When he finds someone who does not have a clue about who she is or where she is going, he figures he has hit the jackpot. He simply can brainwash her into believing that the sky is purple and the moon is pink. Sometimes a woman is so happy to have some attention that it does not matter what is down the road as long as she has someone to tell her lies about what he thinks about her. It sounds good at the time. She is convinced that he is the one to rescue her heart out of bondage. What a sad disappointment.

CHAPTER FOUR
Daddy's Little Girl

Like my mom, I also suffered at the hands of a man. I have been through hell and back. I have also been burned mentally and physically. I too suffer in silence and withdraw just like my mother did at times. Withdrawing from reality did not have anything to do with my biological father. My father is a wonderful man, but he was only around when my mom would let him be after the separation. I know that there are a lot of mothers like that, who get mad at the father for whatever reason and stop his visitation rights illegally. Maybe it's because he has moved on with someone else, or he has no job to help support the child. Whatever the reason, maybe it is not justifiable. Children need both parents in their lives, and to deprive the father of seeing his child is wrong for any reason. Now I must admit that if the father is causing the child any harm, then he should be removed from the child's life. If the father is doing things to the child that are unreasonable, I think that he should be out of the child's life. By the way, when I think of a man doing anything to his children other than love them, I want to just set him on fire. Well, maybe not, but I do want to get my point across. I may sound a little cold, but I believe that I have reason to be. There is no justifiable reason to hurt a child, absolutely no reason at all.

Since my father was not around all of the time, this left me open for sexual abuse by my brother and stepfather. I was abused by my stepfather from the age of five through eleven. He sexually abused me whenever my mom went off to do her jobs. My brother only abused me once or twice. This does not make it right, just because it was once or twice. It should not have even happened. My brother would do stuff like stick his fingers in my butt or rub on my small breast. I guess he was playing house or doctor or whatever it is the kids call it. My mom was so out of it that she didn't have a clue about what was going on around her. She was heavy into drugs and alcohol. She was dealing with her own demons. She was always on the lookout to find the next rock. Drugs and alcohol made her senses very dull. She would be so high and drunk at times that she would be almost be in a trance. My stepfather played on my mom's weakness. It was a free-for-all when my mom was out of her mind. I can remember quite a few times when he would make himself come on me after he masturbated. There are many things I have chosen to forget, but there are some things that just will not leave me alone. I remember being scared to be left alone with him on many occasions because I knew what would happen. He would always wash my young body off and then get on top of me and try to penetrate me. He would do this on a daily basis. He would then kiss me and rub my little vagina with his penis and fingers. He was a big, bad monster that needed to be destroyed by all means necessary. He was a monster that never should have been born. I still think today that he should have been castrated and sent out of the country. He made my life a living hell, and like my mom, I too am destroyed when it comes to relationships and trust. It is very hard for me to reach out and trust because I have been betrayed. I think I suffer sexually because of this sick episode with him. I think that I suffer silently when it comes to sex with another person because I always think back to the sick episodes in my life. Sometimes I may get hooked up with the wrong partner, and through no fault of his, it feels like he is raping me. This is a horrible feeling to have with someone you are being intimate with. I think that my stepfather had some kind of mental illness or something. Anytime you think that you can get your rocks off by screwing a little girl, something has to be seriously wrong with you.

There are so many young ladies who have suffered betrayal by their mothers' boyfriends or husbands. This type of violence should not be allowed in the United States or anywhere. I believe that these men should be castrated and then given a shot in the heart with some acid. This way they will not be able to destroy another child or woman again. There should be tougher laws in place to handle the matter at hand. Nowadays, men are not scared of the justice system. They know that the justice system is a joke. They know that they will get a slap on the wrist and be labeled a sex offender. Some of these men can live with this, as long as they get to have sex with some young tender. Some actually believe that if they sleep with a young girl, it could cure hair loss or other problems of that nature.

My stepfather was really thinking that he was getting away with something when my mom would be too high to remember that she had a daughter in the home. Often he would keep her high just so that he could take advantage of me. Normally when she would get smoked out, she would just fall asleep. He knew this. I hated this part. I can remember that he even invited a friend over to join him in screwing me over. I was so devastated and scared. I grew tired of being used for their sick pleasures, but their strength overpowered mine. I would fight back, but that never worked. They would just laugh and tie my hands up and do whatever they wanted to do. They would put duct tape over my mouth and rape me repeatedly. As I got older, they would try to stick their penises in my mouth many times. I would bite, so that's where they would draw the line. I really tried to protect myself, but I failed so many times. I must stop to take a moment to collect myself. The pain of remembering is too much to bear. I feel like I need to stop talking about this issue because it is just too much for me. Some things I can't even begin to explain without completely losing my mind. Just know that I have been a victim of sexual abuse for a long time. I know exactly what my mom went through silently, and not being able to tell someone, especially your mom, is very hurtful. After all, she is supposed to believe her daughter at all times, even if she thinks what she is telling her is farfetched. Mom, my imagination is wild but not that wild.

I never once had any therapy to heal my mind. I never told anyone, because I thought it was my fault. My mom was in no shape to hear the truth. She was pretty messed up herself. She was fighting demons day and night. I just had to pray for God to give me strength to carry on. I have to admit that I am still suffering from time to time. I just know how to play it off to maintain my sanity. Sometimes when someone does something that is out of line, it takes me back to my past. Like now, I do not like anyone to touch me without permission. I tend to jerk away from them. I do not mean to, but it is just not safe for me to be touched without giving my consent. I have a lot of hang-ups that need to be addressed. I am dealing with them through God's grace and mercy. I often feel sorry for myself because I was so helpless in protecting myself and my mom. I know that I cannot keep beating myself up, but it just hurts so bad. It is very possible that my life might have turned out to be so different if I had not had to endure the pain and agony of sexual violence in my past. I know that is not a guarantee, but I sure would have liked the opportunity to know.

What is so surprising to me is that I almost turned out exactly like my mom, who endured so much sorrow. That would not have been all bad, but some of the things that she endured were unspeakable. I guess you can say that I should not have endured what I did either. But her biological father taking advantage of her was just the worst taboo of them all.

A father is someone we look up to for guidance and protection from the bad and the ugly. The big bad wolf in the woods and so forth. A father is not supposed to display anything other than pure love for his daughter—not lust for his daughter. He is supposed to only have eyes for his wife or girlfriend at the time. There is absolutely no excuse for unethical behavior toward any of his children. If he has suffered himself in the past from sexual abuse, then he needs to seek help before he harms any of his children. I have to admit, some men have suffered at the hands of their fathers, so the pattern goes on and on. No one is seeking help. They just keep going on and on, acting like nothing is bothering them. Actually, sexual abuse is one of their best-kept secrets until someone gets wind of it. A lot of people keep this as a secret because they do not want anyone to think of them differently. This does not justify a damn thing. Be a man and get some damn help if you have suffered silently. Do not hurt your children or wife.

My mom has had to seek counseling on many occasions. She has had two to three nervous breakdowns in the past. She could not bring herself to stop thinking about her past. I reckon that her past was more hurtful than she could withstand. My mom had the strength to love her daddy after a while, but you could tell that the damage was already done. She had enough strength within herself to forgive him. She started going to church, so I believe that this was the reason that she was able to turn the other cheek. Going to church did not stop her demons from visiting her at night when she was trying to sleep. So she would turn to drugs, as I have mentioned before. My mom was on every street drug imaginable, from pills to nose candy. She already had one addiction, and that was the addiction to the life of sleeping with a variety of strange men. When she started doing this, in the beginning it was for money. Later when she started sleeping with strange men, it was for the fun of it. My mother was seeking attention and affection. She had the desire to be touched. She needed this artificial love to be pumped into her veins. Like a critical patient needing oxygen to breathe, my mom needed to be accepted, and if sleeping with strange men would do the trick, then well, so be it. I love my mom so much. At first I was a very bitter young lady because I thought she was just selling me out. It was not that at all; it was because she did not have a clue about raising and protecting a daughter. She was fighting demons herself, so she was in no state to fight and realize what effect this damage would have on me. As I have gotten older, I have learned to forgive my mother. After all, we can't change the past. We can just keep looking to the hills for God's grace and mercy.

CHAPTER FIVE
Single Motherhood

I was at a very young age when I became a mother. I had my first consensual sexual experience at the age of eleven. This was due to peer pressure. My friends wanted me to join the grownup club. They never once told me that sex came with a bundle of joy. I had friends that were already working on their second and third babies. I did not realize how my friends were getting them, but it sure looked like they must have had fun doing it. My mom had warned me of the dangers of having unprotected sex, but my friends were insisting that I go for it. I could not wait to get this sex thing over with so that I could stay in the popular crowd. I had a little guy that I had a crush on anyway. So why not give him a shot at puppy love. His name was Donald, and I had the biggest crush him too. I used to play with his sister all the time. We were really good childhood friends.

I really wish that I could have waited on something that was not that big a deal. It seemed like he knew what he was doing, but I was really not that into him, especially because of my past.

Having sex was not my forte. Well, anyway, I did it, and guess what? It did not mean anything to me. It only reminded me of the sickness I had endured from my stepfather and brother. I went on to play off my dislike. I did not want him to be offended; after all, he could not even begin to understand the hell I had gone through. I guess he was too young to even care what was going on with me.

Having sex with him started a whole new playing field with my peers. It was the cool thing to do. How having sex with someone at such a young age was cool beats the hell out of me. With sex comes emotional baggage. You have to be ready to deal with this aspect of it. I guess that is why you wait until you are married to that someone special before you lie down with them. You are both into each other. It is a beautiful thing when someone cares about you when it is over and done. It is not a one-night-stand, or a drive-by, or a hit-and-run. It is passion between two people who are down for each other. Sex is used for all sorts of things, and I am coming to find this out. People need to take the time out and think about it before they plunge in. I know that this little funny feeling is a wonderful thing to feel. I know that you see the stars and the moon when it comes to the time of explosion. But we really need to take our time in making this very important decision.

I had been having sex for two years before I got caught up. I was thirteen when I conceived my son. Believe it or not, getting pregnant saved my life, because I was hanging with the wrong crowd of people. This forced me to straighten up. I was hanging with people who had bullet wounds and were used up by drugs and people. I was hanging with young women who were working on their second and third child at the age of fourteen. Most of them did not even know where the father was. He abandoned them and the baby. Most of the time the guys would tell you that they loved you in order to get you in the sack. That little trick worked. I really did not have any positive role models to look up to. I did not once judge my friends or turn my nose up at them. These were my friends, who came from broken homes like I did. All we had was each other in the end. We could relate to each other, like gang members relate to each other. We were a clique that hung tough. We wore each other's clothes because we could not afford to get any new clothes on our own. We would sneak out and spend a night over at each other's houses just so we would not have to face what was going on in our homes. I can remember running away from home a couple of times because I did not want to face the music of the reality on Thirty-third and Paseo. I was determined to make a fast getaway from home often.

It was never a question on who my child's father was. Some of my friends had questions about their child's father. Or some of my friends just did not bother to find out the truth, because back in the day, you never really asked questions about who was your baby daddy. You just knew that you were the mother, and that was a good enough explanation. I knew exactly who my baby daddy was because I was paying close attention to him when it happened. It happened on a summer evening when he decided to invite me over for the first time to his uncle's house. I was flattered that this young man would invite me over. I kind of was not expecting to have sex with him at that particular time. I was just planning to hang out with him. I probably should have taken my fast butt home and stopped playing with this man. I can remember him telling me not to move or he was going to come. I knew at that instant that I was going to be in trouble. I knew that it was more than pleasure coming out of this sexual episode. Well guess what? I moved. I must have moved the right way because he surely did have a huge spill right inside of me. When it was over and done, he had the darnedest look on his face. He looked as if he was asking himself, "What have I done?" Well guess what? It was too late, my friend. We had produced something so beautiful yet sinful. My son's father was in his twenties when we had sex. He had told me that he was only sixteen. He had very young features, so I believed him. I did not find out his true age until I filed for child support. I know what you are thinking. You are thinking that he should have been in a jail cell for statutory rape of a minor. He denied to all of his friends that he had even slept with me. He was more ashamed than anything of being found out, but not of the act itself. I can remember how it all happened. He was visiting from Rolling Fork, Mississippi. He was a long way from home, making babies. I do not know exactly how many babies he left behind here. But it was rumored that he had fathered another young girl's child. He was here in Kansas City trying to find a job. He found me instead, a young girl who did not have a clue about anything. All I knew was that this guy was showing me some kind of attention that I desperately needed. I had low self-esteem, no positive guidance, no sense of direction. These things that I lacked made me an easy target.

I did not tell my mother that I was pregnant. I hid the pregnancy for five months. I was so thin and frail that she did not notice until she happened to walk in on me while I was taking a bath. This is when she saw my little pouch sticking out. All she did was gasp and shut the door. She ran to the front room looking for the yellow pages so that she could call the nearest abortion clinic. My mom was so devastated. She was trying to figure out how the hell this happened. It was not like she was paying any attention to me and what was going on around her. If it was not a white substance that could be sniffed, she would not even glance at it. My mom was not trying to hear anything that I was saying. I was trying to tell her who did this, but she had her own ideas. I guess she was doing me like her mother did her. She did not want to hear anything but where and how much it was going to cost to get my baby aborted. She made it very clear that I was not keeping this baby. She said that she could not afford to take care of the both of us. But the funny thing is that she could afford to take care of her nasty habits of buying crack by any means necessary. Sometimes she would sell anything that was not too heavy to carry out of the house. I can remember a time when she sold a television that she was renting to a dope man. She would still make the payments, so that she would not be found out. My mom was really gone on alcohol and drugs. At the time she was beyond help. As a matter of fact, she was not seeking any help.

My mom was insisting that I get the abortion, so she set me up an appointment with the clinic. I ran away because I did not want to have an abortion. I knew that I was too young to take care of my baby by myself, but I did not want to kill my baby. No, I did not have a clue how things would turn out for me and the baby, but I was sure willing to try to take care of us. I could not get my mom to understand that I loved my unborn child and that this would give me a new lease on life. Having a baby would change my life for good, because it was no longer me that I had to care for. It would teach me not to only think of myself. After I ran as far as I could, eventually I ended up going back home to my mom, and she took me straight to the clinic. They examined me and found out that I was way too far along to do the procedure. They said if they did the procedure, then it was going to be very expensive. My mom was not going to let money get in the way of her nose candy. So she came up with the next best thing. She was trying to come up with all kinds of ways to get rid of my baby. I can remember a time that she was so intoxicated that she stood at the top of a flight of stairs behind me and said to me, "I should push your motherfucking ass down the stairs so that baby would just roll out of you." I screamed and cried and ran to the bottom of the stairs, and I ran to my friend's house until the next day when I knew my mom would be slightly sober. My mom was on a whole other level during my pregnancy. Since she could not come up with the money to proceed with the abortion, she was very determined to make my life a living hell the duration of the pregnancy.

I finally got used to being a victim at the hands of my mother. I knew how to deal with her after a while. She kind of got used to the idea at the seventh month of my pregnancy. She enrolled me in the Teenage Parent Center for young mothers. This school was a very good school for young mothers like me. The teachers taught us how to take care of our bodies as well as our new bundle of joy. A lot of the girls were going to have to give up their babies once they were born. Their parents were not having it at all. My mom even thought that this was the way that we were going to go, but I guess I gave her a hell of a fight on that kind of thinking. I had it in my mind that no one was going to take my baby away from me. I was going to do whatever it took to keep my baby. If that meant fighting with my mom every day, then so be it. Also, if that meant having to raise my baby without a father, then I was ready for that challenge also.

I had my beautiful son on March 24, 1986. He weighed in at six pounds and nine and three-quarter inches. He was so amazing to me. He was one of the most beautiful little human beings I had ever seen. I could not believe that I had given birth to someone so special. He was my little miracle, and he still is today. I named him Dwaune. All I could think of was my little baby boy who depended solely on his mother, who was just a baby herself. I was determined to make the best of our situation.

I was not going to let anyone harm him. I would kill anything breathing that even thought of hurting my baby. I guess this is still true today. I will do whatever it takes to keep my baby from harm. My mom was so proud of her first grandchild. It was like she had never thought of getting rid of him. It was like she did not even know where an abortion clinic was. She was walking around like the proud grandma. She even took some time off of sniffing that good-good. I must admit this made a temporary change in her. It was a temporary change, but it was a good one. I was so proud of my baby and myself because I knew that we were solely going to depend on each other for everything. I did not mind sacrificing my life for my son. He is really all I have in the end. He will always be my little miracle who did not know how close he was to being in a nonexisting situation. I am also proud because he has made me a proud mom.

CHAPTER SIX
Moving Out
And Gone For Good

Shortly after I had my son, I moved out of my mom's house, and I have been gone ever since. I was a lost fourteen-year-old who had no sense of direction. I was lost indeed, simply because my mom was lost. We were two lost souls who did not have a clue about life, love, money, and other things. My mom's life was truly a journey that took many twist and turns into darkness. So automatically my life took that same pathway. I started creating habits of self-destruction. I started doing things that got me rewards of food. Yes, I said food. There were times that I was so hungry that I would often eat out of the garbage to survive. My mom was not bringing home any groceries. She was bringing the "Bitch" home on a daily basis instead of nourishment for me and her. The Bitch was the crack in the bottle that would take the best people and make them fall to their knees. The Bitch is responsible for so many broken homes. She comes into a home and destroys everything that looks like it has life and brings it to a slow death. She is a highly favored food for the junkie. She knows that her victim would kill, steal, and destroy for her. She is Satan in a bottle. She ruined my life, and I was not even snorting her. I was always trying to run from her, but she always found her way of catching up to me through my mom. It is a true fact that crack can mess up a whole entire family. You may think it is just the user, but it's not. The user just gets the gratification of being high for approximately fifteen to twenty minutes at a time. If I were to choose drugs, I would be sure to pick one that would take me on a high that lasted longer than twenty minutes at a time. I would take something that would have me high at least for an entire day if I was addicted to anything. I believe in getting your money's worth.

When I moved out, I thought that I had struck gold with Mr. Right. He knew my situation at home with my mom, and he preyed on that weakness. He knew that he could entice me with the many wonderful flavors of food. I guess you can say that it did not take much for me to leave home. I will tell you exactly how he did it. He was at the store one day, and I bumped into him. He was in the produce aisle. I was there trying to see what I could purchase with the five dollars in my pocket, because I knew that I was going have to make it last for the next three days. I was going to piece together a nice meal for me, and I was also trying to figure out how to buy milk for my baby. This young man told me he thought I was cute. See, this is where he got me. I was not used to those kinds of remarks from the opposite sex. He asked me for my number, and it was on from there. He was like my knight in shining armor. He saved me from the drama of being neglected and abandoned. I have to admit, we were moving kind of fast. He asked me to move in with him after we had been dating for only about a month. I thought about it for a few seconds and said, "Sure, why not?" After all, I did not have anything to lose; as a matter of fact, I had everything to gain. I would gain my own space, plenty of food, and my baby some stuff. Little did I know that after a year of living together, this would be too good to be true.

Our first year was a wonderful one. This man took care of me and my son. He treated my son like he was his own. We were such a happy family at the time. This man introduced me to things that I could only dream of. He took me on family trips. His hometown was Canton, Mississippi. And I really liked it there. His family welcomed my son and me with open arms. Finally, I knew what a real family was. Life just could not get any better. I was so happy and in love that nothing could tear my joy down. I finally had the American dream in my grasp. I did not have to look any further for happiness because it was staring right back at me. Now I could finally raise my son up to be the best that he could ever be. I was still in high school when I was dating him. He was driving me back and forth to school, so I no longer was riding the school bus. I had made it to the big times, I thought. Life was very challenging for me back in the late eighties and early nineties.

The second year and so on was full of drama. We grew tired of each other and restless. Mainly it was him growing tired of me and my baby. He was so demanding and critical. He started doing things that were just not to be tolerated by another human being. If things did not go his way, he would throw tantrums like a two-year-old. He grew jealous of my friends and family. He wanted my undivided attention. No one else was supposed to talk to me or look at me. I can remember a time when someone spoke to me; he punched me in the back of the head. This was the first time he had hit me. I was shaken, but not enough to get out of the relationship. After all, my mom never left her men when they hit her. So I guessed I had to stay and hope that he would never hit me again. I learned that, that hit was just the first of many to come. He was always hitting on me. Some days he would just hit on me because he knew that I was not going to do anything about it. It's not that I did not want to do anything about it. It is because I did not have anywhere else to go. I have to remind you that this man was my provider and safe haven. He was my personal bank account. He was my access to food and other necessities for me and my son. I know what you are thinking. You are thinking, were all of these things that he did for me worth the pain and sorrow? I have to say yes, because if you think about where I came from and where I was standing, it was not a hard decision. Besides, I would only hurt for a little bit. I know that this sounds like crazy talk, but this is really how it was.

So many of us get caught up between the things of life instead of our lives. We get caught up with what the man can do for us instead of running as fast as we possibly can. Our minds are fixed on him. The man has some kind of control over us when he knows what it takes to keep us. Yes, ladies, we do sell our souls for the things of this earth instead of realizing we have the power that we need to get out of this kind of abusive relationship. If we just look to the hills, we then can find our strength in Jesus. Sometimes we do not have the courage to run, because we are so worried about our image of staying with the pro athlete, doctor, lawyer, police officer, or other men in general. Our lives are being defined by a man and stuff that he waves in front of us. We are truly sellouts when it comes to being like the Joneses. We will put up with anything just so that we can say, "I have a man too. He may not be any good, but I have one. He may slap me around a few times, but I have a man. He may molest my daughter, but I have a man. He may be sleeping with my best friend, but I have a man. He may not work, but I have a man. He may tell me that I am an ugly Betty, but I have a man." All of these things make us a sellout. Ladies, we need to start thinking more highly of ourselves once we discover that we are about something.

My man was indeed a control freak. He manipulated me into thinking that I would never make it without him. He had me so jacked up that I thought I was the ugliest thing that God could have created. I remember a time when he talked to me so bad that I just knew I would never amount to anything in this lifetime. He also told me that the only thing that was good about me was my sex, and that it was the only way I was going to make it. And I believed him. I just knew he was telling the truth about me. After all, he was a man who knew everything. He would not dare tell me a lie. Actually, I thought of him as a prophet or something, simply because he was always telling me what was going to happen to me if I left him or if I stayed. I guess you can tell that this was not a win-win situation. I loved this man, and I thought he loved me too. But as time went on, I realized that you do not hurt the one you love, and you surely do not beat them into a bloody pulp.

I can remember a time when he beat me so badly that I kneeled on the side of the bed and prayed that God would just take me out. I had had many beatings, but this one was intolerable, maybe because I had not healed up from the other beatings. This particular beating was the first of many to send me to the hospital. We were arguing over some letters that I had found in his pants pocket. He was also drying letters in the oven from some chick in Mississippi. He was falling in love with this girl named Michelle. When I asked him about the letters, he denied that he had a love interest out of town. Whenever he would go out of town, he would not leave me and my son anything to eat. He would hide the food in the ceilings so that we would starve. He would be polite enough to leave us some bread and butter so that I could make us a sandwich. He did not want us to have anything. He locked up everything so that we would suffer while he was out of town. He was a mean bastard. He was sick with hatred. He did not want me, and he did not want to lose me either. Go figure.

As I have mentioned, he beat me so badly that I ended up in the hospital. He snatched me by my collar and punched me in the face. He then tried to bite me. He then kicked me in the chest, and this is when I fell backward and hit my head on the television. He would not stop beating me; he just kept on until he got tired. I was in so much pain that I could not even scream for help. He just kept on and on. I think he was trying to kill me so that he did not have to worry about me or so that no one else could have me. After the bad beating, he had the audacity to want to have sex with me. What is this about? It must be some sick thing behind a man, thinking that you want to have sex with him after he has knocked you senseless. I believe that it's more like rape than just plain sex. He would throw me on the bed and tear my clothes off of me and have sex with my bloody and bruised body. When he came, he just would squirt it all over my wounds like it was medicine or something. Then he would get up and laugh and then take me to the hospital. I would never tell on him, because I did not want him to do anything to my child while I was in the hospital. He was crazy enough to do something like that, so I did not want to take any chances. I would always make up excuses for him. I would tell everyone that I was on medication that made me clumsy from time to time. Of course, many speculated that something else was going on, but I never would tell.

My man had me brainwashed, and he made me feel like I had no control over my life at all. He could be so sweet at times, but when he was mean, he was really mean. We had lived together for approximately six years, not once knowing each other like we should have. The only thing that was keeping me with him was the fact that he helped me raise my son. He was a father to my son. My son's father got out of his life when he was two months old and has been gone ever since. You know I often wonder what makes parents abandon their children. What makes them just up and leave out of their child's life? If you were not forced out, why walk away from your offspring? I guess this is something that I will never understand. Well anyway, this violent man had some kind of love in him somewhere to take my son as his own. Even though I had love for this man, I started to grow tired of the beatings and forced sex. I began to realize that I was someone who had enough courage to make it on her own. It took me a little time, but I got myself together and found a job so that I would not have to be controlled by him when it came to providing for me and my son. I was eighteen when I worked my very first job. I worked at the Hyatt Regency Hotel. I was so happy to finally start making my own money. It may not have been a lot of money, but every little bit helped. When I first started my job, I had only one pair of shoes, one pair of jeans, one shirt, one pair of panties, and one bra. I had lost all of my clothing when my boyfriend had one of his jealous fits. He had thrown all of my clothes out in the trash. I can remember coming home to find people going through my clothing. I was so sad, because it had taken me a long time to accumulate all that I had. He was so cruel to me. I never understood why. How can a person be so mean to another person for no reason at all? I know that I did not deserve any of the violence that he placed upon me. I was just looking for love, since I could not get any at my mom's home. It was nothing but pure trickery when he wanted me to move out of my mom's house. He thought he had a daughter instead of a young lady who loved and appreciated him for caring so much about me and my son.

CHAPTER SEVEN
Self-Esteem

I had worked at the Hyatt Regency Hotel for ten years. This was really good for my first job. I had it made, and I knew how to take care of myself and my baby. I still had this man controlling my every move. Often he would make sure that I came straight home, and he would make sure that I didn't spend money before I came home. He was starting to control how much I could spend and how much of my check he could have. I think that I stood up for myself after a while. I did not mind helping out with the bills, because I believe that a person should pay where they lay. I never have had a problem with helping. He just made it hard. I think he got off on making my life a living hell. It was all about him and not us. The more I worked, the more he could see that he had to loosen the grip that he had on me. I started realizing that I could do better all by myself. I started working all of the overtime that was offered to me. My paychecks got better and better. The better the check got, the higher my self-esteem rose. I got higher and higher on life.

I was so high on life whenever I worked. I found out that my strength was in my working. I noticed that whenever I worked, I could take my mind off the drama at home. I would often cry when it was time to clock out. People would ask me why I wasn't happy to be going home? I would often tell them that I did not want to go home. I never told them why; I just told them that someone was sick and I had to take care of him. This way they would stop asking questions. I often took my time in going home, because I knew what was on the other side of the door waiting to make my life a living hell. I would often fall into my own little imagination, thinking that things were getting better. This imagination helped me to cope with Mr. Hell-raiser. I never could understand what made him so possessive and angry. It seemed like everything I did to make him happy was making him angry. It's like he hated me with a passion. I never would be good enough for him. This is what he was telling me on a daily basis. He would tear my self-esteem down every chance he got. He made me feel like I was a nobody. He would often tell me that I was ugly and fat and no one wanted me unless I would suck their dicks, and all I was good for was a good fuck. Oh yeah, baby, he was raw, just like that. He made me believe that I had nothing else going on for me. I had no smarts, no talent, no nothing: just a bitch who amounted to nothing but a wet ass. He made me feel so small at times. I knew that these things had to be true because anyone who loves you must be telling the truth, right? I knew he must have known the truth about me, because his beliefs about me were like the Bible, right? He had me thinking that I was not a good mother because I chose to work for a living. He told me that my child would grow up to disrespect me and then hate me because I was working. He had me believing that by working and bettering myself I would die somehow. He basically had me tripping over some bullshit. As I sit back and think about this, I must pause, because I have become very emotional. There was no reason to be so mean to me. I am one of the nicest people that one could ever come in contact with. I am a true humanitarian . I do my best to make people feel comfortable when they are in my presence. I do my best to make sure people get an encouraging word from me before they leave my side. Despite all the beatings, I still managed to turn out to be the very best that I could be. Sometimes it amazes me how well I turned out, simply because I had a man who tore me down at every chance he got.

CHAPTER EIGHT
My Addictions

Even though I was dealing with low self-esteem and other bullshit in my life, I still managed to cope very well. It had to be the grace of God that was pulling me through. It had to be him carrying me through all of my pain and sorrows of this cruel life. Certain things just would not leave me alone. There were demons and mean people that would get a pleasure out of seeing me tumble and fall flat on my face. I never understood how a person could get so much gratification from seeing another person fail. Like they say, misery loves company, and if people see that you are too happy, they feel intimidated by your joy. So they feel that they have to come by and destroy your happiness with one stroke of cruelty. Some people just do not realize that they can be just as happy if they try really hard to be. Happiness starts within. You and only you can make you happy. You cannot depend on another to make you happy. You will only be faced with disappointment from time to time. I had to learn this the hard way. I have learned the secret of happiness through the strength of Jesus Christ. He is my power and strength through it all. Through good and bad, he is my source of power. Even though I knew how to make myself happy and content with the things that I had, I still fell victim to the A word. This was my downfall that lasted until I was thirty-six. I was not aware that this thing I was going through was an addiction that was destroying me piece by piece.

I first recall that I started having a strange taste for a different kind of food whenever I would get hurt mentally or physically by someone. I noticed that I started developing an appetite for this kind of strange fruit that just tasted so damn good to me every time I would take a big bite. I would just close my eyes and let my tongue taste all the senses of the juices of this wonderful fruit. This fruit was something that you could not buy at any supermarket; you could not even grow it on trees. This fruit was created from the heavens. You would think that anything created from the heavens would not be so harmful when ingesting too much of it, but unfortunately, this fruit is very harmful to your health if you take it without knowing the dangers of eating too much of it. At times this fruit can be really good for your health, and at other times it can kill you. Sometimes you can die in an instant, or you can die a slow and painful death when eating this wonderful fruit that was created from the heavens. You have to be really careful of your bites into this fruit; it may be the beginning or ending of you and your whole self-esteem. This fruit I am speaking of is the *men* in our lives. Yes, I would run to this type of fruit whenever I would be hurt by others.

I am not sure why exactly I never chose to keep taking real drugs to ease the pain that I was going through. I used to think that I was grownup with my friends whenever we would smoke a little weed every now and then. This was the thing to do back in the day. Like I've mentioned before, peer pressure is a booger. I used to try everything I could to ease the pain of my life. It was normal to try a variety of things with your friends. It was not always the best thing to do, but it would ease the pain of reality on a given day. Sometimes I sit back and wonder which is worse: being on drugs for a lifetime or getting your heart broken over and over again. Sometimes if you are courageous and a daredevil, you may try to mix the two, but that can be a dangerous cocktail. You have one that makes you feel wonderful when brought into the secret of the darkness, and you have one that you meet and greet and then you two become lovers and so forth. Which one are you willing to sacrifice your soul for? You may or may not notice that you are addicted to this drug of choice until it is too late. You may already be so far gone that it is going to take an intervention to bring you back to your senses. My intervention was a divine intervention. It came like a thief in the night. Something horrible happened to me that was unspeakable. Well, it kind of already had been happening; I just did not care to notice that my life was no longer mine. It was everyone else's, including my variety of addictions. I had no sense of identity. I no longer knew who I was or what I wanted. All I knew is that I wanted what everyone wanted me to have or be.

I no longer could think on my own. I was slowly dying, and I did not even have a clue that I had developed a need to feed my issues. I did not even realize that I was in ICU on life support. This is what addicts never realize—that they are in need of help but refuse to seek any until it is too late for them and they have destroyed their lives beyond recognition. I found out an addict is really someone who gets hooked on drugs, alcohol, and whatever has their undivided attention by all means necessary. This could come in the form of a man, rolled up, snorted, and inhaled, in a glass, in a pipe, or anything that can manipulate you into thinking that you need it and that you cannot live without it. It brainwashes you and takes control of you in every way possible. It gets very expensive to be an addict. You would think that addicts would not lose anything if they already do not have anything, but unfortunately, this is not true. We addicts lose everything when we are lost in the world. We lose our family, friends, jobs, houses, and anything that connects us to others.

When I was an addict, I could not tell if I was losing or gaining. I could not distinguish between the two. At times I felt as if I was gaining, because my needs were being met on all levels. I was not aware of my losses until I woke up one day and found out that Shelle was no longer the person she was so many years ago. She was a puppet, and people took her kindness for weakness. I have noticed that if you are weak, you tend to have more people using you, but when you are strong, people want to fight with you all the time. They want to test you on a given day. Actually, a lot of people secretly hate you for the fact that you have so much strength. This has always puzzled me. Why do people hate you so much when you are trying to better yourself? Some people treat you miserably because they do not have the courage or the strength to make things better for themselves, so they do their best to destroy what you are all about.

My addiction started at the age of sixteen. At this age I was also suicidal. I was going through so many episodes of life at such a young age. I never knew that life could be so hard on a young person. When I was going through my journey of life, I must have picked up some of my mother's habits as well as creating some of my own. I always have found myself looking for someone to love me unconditionally. Even though I say this, I could not even recognize it when someone was really being real with me. I always thought these men that came across my path were really down for me. They would at least act like they were down with me, without any strings attached. I would fall for the okeydokey many times. I did not even once realize that they were only pleasing me so they could gain something from me. That never crossed my mind. I guess it never crossed my mind because I was young and naive. I thought everyone that smiled at me was my friend. Well, it took years before I finally realized that this was really not true. I figured out if they are smiling at you, you'd better be watching their eyes too. You'd better just look into their souls and see if they really mean well. It took me so many trials to realize that I really do not have that many friends after all. I just have a few people who expect something from me, regardless of whether I have it or not. Being an addict, I thought I had a lot of people looking out for my best interest. I thought that they were looking out for me whenever I could not look out for myself. But little did I know that they were silently destroying me by any means necessary. They did not care whether I lived or died. They cared about the benefits of hanging and kicking it with me. They knew I would eventually fall asleep and then they could rob me of everything that I was building. The sad thing is that I trusted these people to take good care of me if I were taking care of them, but they didn't. I thought I was always making my life better when I would come into a man's presence. I thought that he would never run game on me, because he knew that I was the weaker sex. I thought that he would acknowledge the fact that I was like a fragile newborn that needed love, protection, and nourishment. I thought that he would acknowledge that I, like many other women, was a gift from God. Why would he harm or use someone who was given to him by the Almighty? Why not accept his blessing and be proud that God thinks of him enough to give him this woman? I do know for a fact that God takes away blessings if you mistreat them. I know for a fact that he will not keep blessing you if you are not taking care of your blessings like you are supposed to. He will destroy the blessing and give it to someone who really needs it. It is amazing that you never know what you have until it's gone. I have often wondered why people have to lose something before they know that it was possibly the best thing for they, and they just let it slowly disappear before their very eyes. How sad is this?

CHAPTER NINE
I Am Still Suffering

I have suffered for so many years at the hands of men. I often wondered why we were created if the ones that we were created for mistreat us and run game on us all the time. Why are we around if they do not really want us around? Why do they play so many mind games? Why do they leave us behind when we are the mothers of their children? Why do they hit or beat us into a bloody pulp? Just why do they do the things that they do to us? I often hear the response that "men are only doing what we allow them to do." I beg to differ. We are not allowing them to keep hurting us over and over again. We are just trying to love them and care for them. As a matter of fact, we are doing our parts. We are doing our jobs that God has put us on this earth for. But they on the other hand, they have some kind of sick and twisted ideas about how we should be treated. Even though I am recovering from my many addictions, I still often feel like I am going through a relapse from time to time. I feel like I need to pick this fruit up and just eat it until I am completely full, but something in me tells me that I'd better not or I will lose everything that I have accomplished. I never want to be in that situation again, where I don't know if I am coming or going. I do not want that feeling of being lost again. It is a lonely and scary feeling when your soul is lost. You do not know where to go or who to trust when you can't find your own way.

I often find myself talking to other women and find out that we have a lot in common when it comes down to the men in our lives. We are just trying to figure out how to make it through the pain and joys of having them around us. I know we are always hoping that they will acknowledge that we are human beings, with hearts and emotions that are very sensitive. We are depending on them to take us and love us back. We are expecting them to be there for us mentally and financially.

Basically, we are looking for you to be there. You are our security blanket that no shield should be able to pierce. We are looking for you to understand us and be patient with us. I know that we are very different from each other and that a lot of times you do not know how to handle us, but you have to realize that we are always willing to teach you how to handle us. You never ask us how we feel and what we are thinking. Do you really care? Some of you say that we are just saying the same thing over and over again. This is where I think we start to break down on our communication with you. If you feel that we are saying the same thing over and over again, then you need to sit back and listen carefully, because we may be telling you that we can't take anymore and we are leaving without looking back. We often do get enough courage to walk away, whether you believe it or not. When we get tired of everything, there is nothing that you can say or do to keep us. When we are broken down to our core, there is nothing that can repair us. The only way that we can be repaired is to move on to the next man, hoping and praying that he does not rip our hearts out. My heart is currently bandaged up, with wires and sticks. My heart has been ripped out and thrown in the air and shot forty times. When I hurt like this, it's not a good thing. I start developing a hatred for the likes of any man. I start to keep my guard up and think about ways of hurting you back. I start to think about ripping your heart out and burning it beyond recognition. I start to think of stuff like taking your brains out and feeding them to the dogs. I know this sounds kind of cruel, but this is how I often think when I am hurt by you. I am silently plotting against you because I know you must eventually go to sleep. Now this sounds really suspicious, doesn't it? You never know what a woman is thinking about. We are heavy thinkers, and we often do the things that we are thinking about. So please be careful how you treat your woman. She may be plotting against you while you are just living without a care. Just be careful: we have gotten stronger and more creative when it comes to you. As a matter of fact, we have sat back and watched you and your behaviors, and without you realizing it, we have mastered your behaviors. You are just too silly to realize it. I am not only talking your woman at home; I am also talking about the woman that you run to when home is too hot for you. We are all capable of hurting you and destroying you beyond recognition. A slight change in us may indicate that you are treading in deep waters. A slight change in us means that there is trouble headed your way. The more you hurt us, the more we hate you. The same woman that loves you can destroy you, have you begging for mercy. You may laugh and say "whatever," but this is a true fact. When we have had enough of your bullshit, we turn into these strange beings that we do not even recognize ourselves. My advice to you is to treat us with love and respect, and then you will never have to see this side of us.

I know that all the things that I am saying may be cruel, but it's the truth. We are just as capable of hurting you the way you are hurting us. Some of you think that since we are the weaker sex, that we are worthless. Just think of the black widow and see how dangerous she was. This is food for thought for you unbelievers. We are really sweet until you piss us off. Once you take us there, we will never look at you the same way again. We may have you around us, but we are always looking out the corner of our eyes, watching and making sure you do not get us first. I know that this is not the way to be, but this is an act of survival for some of us. We start out trusting and respecting you, and then we turn around and despise and hate you for breaking us down. We just want to know that you are capable of loving us and caring for us. We just want to know that you need us like we need you.

I just try to stay focused and stay in prayer that I will not have to come to these kinds of twists and turns of a love/hate relationship. I often try to stay positive until I am forced into a negative situation. I can be your friend until the very end. I can be your enemy for an eternity if you take me there. I guess what I am saying is, please do not push me. Please do not make me change into this monster that you've created. I am normally a gentle spirit, but lately I have been feeling like a warrior in a battle. I constantly feel like I am not being heard and taken seriously. I am always trying to prove who I am to you, and you feel as if you do not have to prove yourself to me. What kind of justice is that? I really must apologize; I really do not mean any harm to you. I just want a little TLC and gentleness and kindness from you. Acknowledge that I was created to be by your side. I was not created to be abandoned by you mentally or physically. Some of you get it, and some of you do not care to get it. One thing is for sure: We love you so much. We care for you so much. We accept you in whatever condition you may be in. We accept your imperfections. We accept your cruelty at times. We know that we do not deserve that, but we will put up with you anyway. How is it that you cannot do the same for us? Some of you are very brave to love us, and we appreciate that. On the other hand, some of you are not worth a grain of salt. You are like a car with no tires or like a house with no walls. You are pathetic. It's not that you do not know any better; it is that you just choose not to do any better by us. Just stop for once and think about what you are doing and whose heart you are tearing out. You need to think of your mother when you think about ripping us to shreds. Think about how you would feel if someone made your mother unhappy every time you looked around. This would make you want to kill the man that is causing her so much grief.

I know that some of you are thinking that I have lost my mind and I am out of control, but I am just as sane as you. I am speaking up for the women who can't speak for themselves. I am speaking up for the women who wish they could let you know how they really feel, but they are scared of running you off. If they knew their value, they would not be afraid of you. But since you guys play on our weakness, some of us are scared to death to be lonely without the likes of you. We have brainwashed ourselves into thinking that we are going to die without you. We really think that the world is going to stop spinning when you stop wanting to be with us. Some of us think that we will never get anywhere without you. We think that we will never find anyone else who loves or cares for us. We fall into this dark hole where there is no light to be found. You can't even see your hands in front of your face, because the hole is so dark. Have you ever been in that dark spot? Have you ever been that hopeless? Have you ever been in despair? You almost feel as if you need to get some counseling because of all of the pain that you are going through. You feel as if you are going to have to seek some painkillers to ease the pain, because you have gotten to the point where you can't eat, sleep, or function, period. You are in bad shape. It feels like someone has run over you with a semitruck over and over again. If you ever have been here, then seek help. If you have been blessed to not go through these things, then congratulations; keep up whatever it is that you are doing and share with the rest of us what your secret is. Maybe you should write a book and tell the rest of us what we should do to stay out of harm's way. Show us how to recognize the bad seeds that are in sheep's clothing. Show us how to make it through without all of the games that people play when they are trying to gain something from you, instead of keeping it real with you in the beginning. Some of you know that I am telling the truth; we need to start speaking up about how we are feeling. Do not silently suffer without saying a word. That does not solve anything; it just makes you more and more depressed. It is time to live and seek everything that you desire with the help of prayer. Let go and let God. This is a phrase that helps me whenever I feel as if I am struggling with someone. You should try it. It actually works.

CHAPTER TEN
I Trade In My Life

Through all of the emotional pain and sorrow of my life, I have decided to trade in my life. I have decided that I can't fix and solve all of the problems that come my way. We often think that we can take all of our issues into our own hand without even praying about it. We think that we know everything, and we do not want anyone telling us anything. We walk around with so much pride. Some things could be literally killing you, but just because of your pride, you seek no help. What good is it to walk around like everything is okay when you can just look to the hills and ask for some help? This may sound strange to some, but calling out to the hills is your secret weapon against the devil. After all, we know for a fact that it is the devil's job to destroy. His job is for us to stumble on every corner in the journey of our lives. His job is to distract us from everything that we love. He wants us to lose focus on our goals so that we can be a failure to our own selves. The devil is like a thorn in your side. He is like a cancer that eats and eats away at your life.

If you are not careful, he will seduce you into believing that he is the way to go, simply because he can give you all the things that your flesh desires. Your flesh may desire money, sex, and drugs instead of love. Now, I am not saying that wanting these things are bad; I am just saying that the way you receive these things depends on which way your path is going. You may be headed into a positive direction or a negative direction. I know some things and situations may drive you into doing something that may not be ethical, but hey, some people feel like they have to do what they have to do. Some people do what they need to do; believe it or not, this is a fact in a lot of situations.

This is kind of how my life was, and as a matter of fact, still is. I have had a lot of twist and turns. Some of the things that I am going through are so mystical at times. I do not know whether to keep going through or just sit still until the situation comes to a complete stop. I often ask for advice from my friends to see what kind of knowledge they have about some of the things that I am going through. Most of the time they try to help me stay positive and upbeat, but then other times they can't help me, because they are going through the same issue. It's kind of like the blind leading the blind. Some of the things that I go through are very great learning tools. I have always been the one who has to have the hands-on learning. Things tend to stick with me better when I learn through experience. I imagine that there are a lot of things that one would rather not go through to get the message. Some things can literally kill you if you do not learn from them. It is like bumping your head a thousand times over and over again until you drift out of consciousness. This is the time when you need to kneel down and stay in prayer. Staying in prayer keeps you under the many blessings that God has for you. He is your protector in all of your circumstances if you just believe and call on him. I have learned to call on him for everything, and when I do, he answers. It may not be right away, but it is always on time. I must stop at this point and say, "Thank you, Jesus" for all of the blessings that are given unto me.

From time to time I have to stop and give him thanks. I do not give him thanks only for the good things. I give him thanks for all the trying things too. Once you have traded in your life for him, you will know exactly what I am talking about. You may not get it right now, but you will once you decide to believe that there is someone up above greater than you and the things that you possess. This brings me to a point. So many people believe in the material world that they can't even begin to see the spiritual world. As a matter of fact, they can't see past anything that they can't touch or smell. This is so sad to me when I find out that one of my own is caught up in the world and what the world can do for them. The things of the world are so temporary, yet this is what we have to honor. What happens when these things are taken from us? We lose our minds. We forget that the thing that we cherished so much could be replaced with better and bigger objects. We get depressed over little things like a car, house, job, and anything that will have you tripping. If it helps any, you know that sometimes we lose things so that they can be replaced with new blessings. I guess you can say it is like a blessing in disguise. Sometimes you have to get rid of the old in order to be blessed with the new and improved. Now which one would you prefer? I often ask myself that same question. I have accepted the fact that when things are taken from me, there is something else on the way. I may cry a little for my loss, but I eventually get myself together and get ready to accept my new blessings. I am always very excited when I am about to be blessed.

I heard a pastor say, "God will bless you when he knows that you know how to worship the blessings you already have". See, if you do not take care of the blessings that you already have and you neglect them, you will not receive blessings like you should. Then you often wonder, *Why is everyone doing better than me?* Well it's because you do not know the secret to get the blessings you deserve. Trust me: when you get to the point of despair and disgust, you will see what I am talking about. When you get tired of living like you are living, you will start praying and asking for help. This is exactly what has happened to me. I got so tired of my life going in a crazy direction. I got tired of my life just taking off without me. I often would end up in places that were unspeakable. I would often end up in beds that were not mine or my husband's. I would often end up in dark places, so dark that I could not even see my hands in front of my face. I would often abuse the ones around me because I figured that they would not understand my plight. They would not understand my pain and sorrow. I used to shut a lot of people down before they would get too close to me. I did not want people getting too close, because they would eventually figure out that I was sick and out of my mind. And if this would get out, they would destroy me. My mind was on its own little journey. I faked people out so that they would not know the truth about their sweet little Shelle. If people knew that I had sores of disaster, they would not even speak to me. Because they would have thought I was a monster. I kept my sores of ugliness well hidden. I am just now trying to get rid of the sores of my life. I have been in constant prayer that I heal from my mind to the bottom of my feet. I need to stay under the blood at all times, because if I do not, then things can go so wrong. There are people out there waiting for me, so that they can continue to destroy me beyond recognition. I realize that I used to be a horrific monster, but it is time for a change, and in order for me to change, I must change my surroundings and friends that were poison to my soul. If you ever stop and notice, you will have friends as long as you stay the same person, and as soon as you start to change, your circle of friends gets smaller and smaller. This is a good thing because this means that you are definitely changing. Change is very good, despite what others say about change. Change encourages growth. You want to grow in the right direction. If you do not know the power of change, you will never grow to your full potential. If you choose to stay the same day in and day out, you will never know how far you can go.

I am so determined to change in every aspect of my being. I am determined to be what God has placed me on this earth to be. There are going to be a few people who will stop at nothing to make me stumble and fall. I have learned that people hate to see you get ahead; they hate to see you moving full speed ahead, especially if you are doing it with a smile. I am so happy that I finally got it. I finally got the fact that I need to stay focused and stay positive at all times. I know now that in order for me to be happy, I must not depend on anyone else but me. If you wait on someone else to make you happy, then you are going to be sadly disappointed, every time. A lot of people do not realize this, that self-fulfillment is the key to a happy and positive person. Also you must be a humanitarian and not selfish when it comes to helping your fellow man. You must be a giver to a certain extent; do not give your last, but do give sparingly. I know some of you are saying that is some bull. Some of you do not know how to give, or better yet, some of you do not want to give even if you have it. When I give, I give to those that I feel need my help after they have done all that they can do. I used to just give help just because I had it to give, but then I sadly realized that people will start using you. I have gotten so caught up like that many times. Now I am really careful about who I help. I give because that is one of the requirements of being a changed person. It is a necessity to bless others just like you have been blessed, in order to keep your blessing coming through. I call it the blessing rainbow. Having a rainbow full of blessings is like waking up to angels every day.

CHAPTER ELEVEN
It's Like An Epiphany

Something happened to me this year that made me realize that I needed to figure my life out quick, fast, and in a hurry. If you recall earlier in the book, I was telling you all of my woes and addictions that I was suffering through. Well this particular thing that happened to me was like an epiphany. It was like a semitruck running right through a building. It was like a plane landing in the wrong city. I was so devastated to the point where I had to kneel down and pray for immediate help. I was hurting so bad that I just could not believe that pain could feel like this. I was hurting so bad that I did not know which direction to go. I did not know whether to run or stay still; all I could do was just cry from a broken heart. My heart was broken beyond repair. I was so in a state of shock that it made me realize that I deserved better. I finally realized that I'd had enough of people's bullshit. I'd had enough of living with the fact that I thought I needed people in my life to sustain my existence. I finally realized that I can't be nice to some people, for the simple fact that they will not appreciate me in the end. As a matter of fact, people like that will often start to believe that you owe them something. What a joke. But, baby, the one who is going to get the last laugh is me.

I remember my pain like it was yesterday. It was actually August 14, the weekend of the Hoodie Awards in Las Vegas. The Hoodie Awards is a big event hosted by Steve Harvey, the well-known comedian. Well anyway, this was the first awards show that I'd ever attended. I had always heard about it but was always working when the awards show would go to Las Vegas. This year I was fortunate to make it. I was very excited because not only was I going to get a chance to go to my favorite city in the world, but I was going to be staying at the Mandalay Bay with my sweetie. We both work two jobs, so it is very hard to get that one-on-one time with each other. So I thought this would be an opportunity for us to connect. He works between 60 and 70 hours a week. I work approximately 110–120 hours a week. So you can see where our time is very limited. As we were preparing for our trip, I should have known that it was going to be a disaster because things were a little shaky; he kept on playing mind games. He kept saying he was going, and then he would say that he was not going. He was beginning to drive me crazy. I just knew we weren't going, but we eventually made it.

We boarded the plane with no problem. He was very excited once we were on the plane, and even I was excited. I just knew that once we landed, things would be like a honeymoon. I gave

him his birthday gift of a thousand dollars on the plane. He
was really happy, and he looked over at me like he loved me. I
knew that this was only a temporary love due to the fact that he
had just received money and all-expenses-paid trip. I guess you
can say I bought me some love for that weekend. It is a shame
what we will do for a little company. I have been guilty of this
for quite a long time. I have never required anyone to treat me
with such kindness. Now that I sit back and think about it, that
is so sad. Well anyway, we landed, and he was in awe of the city
and the hotel. He thought he was in a complete paradise. He
was so happy and mesmerized by all of the things that Vegas
had to offer. I guess not having to pay for anything made the
trip even better. My man was good for the first three hours,
and then it went downhill for me. But life was very good for
him. He was like a kid in the candy store who had a choice of
every kind of candy that he could imagine. The candy of choice
was the all of the pretty ladies of all walks of life. I knew that
his head might turn once or twice. I did not have a clue that he
would forget about who he went up to Vegas with. As a matter
of fact, he just completely turned on me. He started acting like
he flew himself up to Las Vegas, and he tricked himself into
believing that he could take one of those pretty little ladies in
the room with him, but there was one problem. The problem
was that he had a woman who was already with him and in love
with him who had just brought him out for his birthday. Now
tell me what the hell is that all about? How can a person be so
cruel to someone so nice? How can a person be so into himself

and not think about anyone else? How is it that a person can lust for things that he knew that he could not have?

I thought that we were going to be as carefree as possible. I thought this trip was for us. I thought that this trip was for us to love on each other, since we do not get a chance to love on each other back at home because of our busy schedules. This brother just completely lost his mind when it came to the other eye candy walking around. He would not hold onto me; he would not even kiss on me. He would do all of these things behind the closed doors. He would not show any kind of affection for me, even when we were at the events. He would not dance with me, because he did not want people to know that we were together. I think this is the part where I finally realized that this man was from someplace unknown. This man was not for me; he did not even deserve someone of my magnitude. He did not deserve someone as nice as I was. He deserved someone who treated him like shit and did not give a damn about him or his feelings. He deserved someone who would make his life miserable like he had made mine. I did not have the strength to do it, because I was in agony. I was just crying and crying to the point that I could not see, because my eyes were swollen shut. We were only there for the weekend, but it felt like we were there for years. This man took me from happiness to sadness in a matter of five hours. I felt like my heart was ripped out and shot into the air. I felt as if he were going to beat the hell out of me at any given minute. There is no way that I should have felt like this when I was expecting us to be a much happier couple. I often ask myself what went wrong and how it went wrong. How did I subject myself to such hate and such a negative attitude? I am not sure how that happened, but it is kind of like a blessing in disguise. Now I know what I need and I do not need in my life. I know now that I need to watch the attitudes of many. They may be nice to you as long as they are getting something out of you, and then when they do accomplish their goal of getting what they want from you, they turn around and mistreat you and then act as if they do not even know who you are. What is up with that? This trip was not going as I had planned. It should have been a pleasurable trip. It should have been a trip that felt like a honeymoon instead of a funeral. I felt like I lost everything that I loved in a matter of minutes. You know the feeling you have when someone passes away or the feeling of losing something that was of great importance to you in a matter of minutes. It was kind of like living the life of a millionaire, and then in seconds you turn into a homeless person. This is exactly how I felt when my vacation went from joy to disaster. This man of mine was a like a perfect stranger whom I had just met. He disappointed me in the worst way. He had the time of his life in Las Vegas. He was so happy to be a part of the crowd. He actually thought of himself as a celebrity that had no time for the likes of me. Wow, every time I think of that, I just get sad, because I will always remember the pain I felt.

This is where I had to find the strength in the hills to survive this madness. I had to cry to the Lord and ask him for all kinds of help, anything to keep me from jumping out of the twenty-fifth-floor window of the Mandalay Bay Hotel. Yep, I was just that damn sad. I felt as if I could jump and be rid of my pain in an instant. Well anyway, I started praying harder than I had before. I eventually started to feel slightly better as the days went on, but I was still shedding tears on a daily basis. There was nothing that I could do to keep my tears in. So I just pretended to be crying from my allergies. It is not like he noticed anyway. His head was in the clouds, while mine was in the hand of Jesus. It was like a constant battle between me and him. I just could not believe the agony I was going through when we were supposed to be happy. I knew I had to pull myself together so that my whole entire trip would not be a complete disaster. The prayers were starting to work, because I started seeing the light on my last day in Las Vegas. I started feeling like I could breathe again. I started feeling like I was on my way to glory days. I had finally seen the light. My epiphany had finally arrived. I knew now that I had to make a decision that would change the rest of my life. I knew that I was going to be finally free from someone who was attempting to destroy me. Now I had the power to move forward. I now see my future in a brighter and brighter light. Now whenever I see that my world is going to be shadowed with darkness, I stop, turn around, and walk the other way. Now I know that if you can't respect who I am or what I am about, then you keep it moving. I live in a positive bubble; I reject negativity on the spot. Negativity is like a form of darkness that I would rather be far away from. I know at times it must come in order for you to be a better person, but it can also destroy you completely beyond recognition. Positivity is like the light of the heavens. This is where and how I direct my paths from here on out. So the lessons of being hurt were not all too bad. The experience made me a better person. It made me aware of my feelings and my sense of being. It is really a sad shame that it takes all the hell and pain for us to finally get it. For us to finally figure out that we are someone and that we deserve someone to love us back in the same manner that we do them. We should not be the only ones trying to walk down the highway. It takes two to make a relationship work. This is very hard for some of you to realize because you do not know your true value. But once you figure it out, you will be better off. Your quality of life will be much better once you get it all figured out.

CONCLUSION
Life Is A Lesson

Life has been truly a journey for me. I have been through any kind of pain that one could imagine. I have been through the sexual abuse, the physical abuse, and the mental abuse. All of the abuse that one could ever go through has in a strange way made me stronger. I have learned that my addictions were bringing me down, man by man. Some of them were down with me; others were only with me because they wanted to use me for their own selfish benefit. I thought they were in a relationship with me to help me. But to my surprise, they were only in the game of love because they were getting paid to do so. I did not realize that they were using me like they were at a part-time job. Some of them were so cold; they would even get money from me to give to other females. This was a very heartless thing to do, but I allowed it to happen over and over again. This is the reason you need to have your self-esteem in check, because if you do not, then you will start to fall for anything or anyone. You will just be so happy that someone is even spending any time with you. You will almost do anything to make this person happy, without realizing that this person may be using you. Once you get your self-esteem in check, you will be a much better person. You will finally see the light. You'll finally acknowledge that the one that matters most is you. It is a wonderful feeling when you figure this out. I feel so much better about who I am. I now know that I must think about me first and then someone outside of me. The roles used to be reversed. I would always put myself last. I thought that being a humanitarian meant to forget all about myself and please everyone else. I see now that is not the case. You must be your own provider, your own protector, your own financial advisor, and your own cheerleader. You must know how to make yourself happy. There is a secret of how to do this simple task. You must pray for all of your needs and then believe that they are going to be fulfilled. This is how I found true happiness. I know that anything that ails me can be resolved through prayer. Amen.